Copyright © 2023 Samantha Pretto

3. Ensuring longevity: Products and techniques.
4. Emergency fixes.

VI. Skincare Before the Wedding
1. Skincare routines based on skin type.
2. Facials: Which ones and how often?
3. Addressing skin concerns: Acne, pigmentation, etc.
4. The role of diet and hydration.

VII. Makeup Styles
1. Makeup through history: Iconic bridal looks.
2. Contemporary bridal makeup styles:
   - Natural
   - Glamorous
   - Vintage
   - Cultural/traditional
3. Makeup based on themes and seasons.

VIII. Makeup Trials
1. The need for multiple trials.
2. Documenting each look.
3. Allergies and sensitivities: Patch testing.
4. Adjusting based on feedback.

IX. Day-of Makeup
1. The importance of priming.
2. Foundations: Matching and longevity.
3. Eye makeup: From shadow to lashes.
4. Lips: Long-lasting choices.
5. Final touches: Highlighting, contouring, and setting.
6. Emergency touch-ups.

X. Professional Help vs. DIY
1. Benefits of hiring professionals.

2. Cost factors.
3. DIY: Tutorials, courses, and practice.
4. DIY vs. Professional: A comparative analysis.

XI. Post-Wedding Care
1. Haircare after heavy styling.
2. Makeup removal: Do's and Don'ts.
3. Skin rejuvenation.

XII. Expert Interviews
1. Hairstylists: Tips and tricks.
2. Makeup artists: Insights on products and techniques.
3. Dermatologists: Healthy skin advice.

XIII. Star Bridal Hair and Makeup Inspirations

XIV. Conclusion
- Emphasizing the bride's individuality.
- Last-minute checklist.
- Well wishes.

I. Introduction

- The Importance of Bridal Hair and Makeup

Every bride embarks on a unique journey towards her wedding day, weaving dreams of timeless elegance with aspirations of contemporary flair. At the heart of this odyssey is the quest for that perfect look—a radiant reflection of her essence, amplified by artful beauty touches. As the canvas of love is set against the backdrop of festivity, the brushstrokes of hair and makeup become crucial players in narrating a bride's individual story. This guide, a harmonious blend of star-studded inspirations and expert insights, seeks to be every bride's trusted companion on this transformative voyage. Dive deep into a world where historical styles merge with modern trends, and personal preferences dance with expert recommendations. Welcome to your bridal beauty symphony, where every note resonates with grace, charm, and timeless allure.

For many brides, their wedding day is a culmination of dreams, hopes, and meticulous planning. Every detail, from the venue to the decor, plays a part in creating a memorable experience. Within this grand tapestry, the bride herself becomes the focal point. Naturally, her appearance, including her hair and makeup, is of utmost importance. But why does bridal hair and makeup carry such weight? Let's explore the multifaceted significance of bridal beauty.

1. A Reflection of Personal Identity:

At its core, bridal hair and makeup is deeply personal. It isn't merely about looking good; it's about reflecting a bride's identity. Some brides opt for glamorous Hollywood waves and bold makeup to exude sophistication, while others might choose a simple bun and minimal makeup to reflect an understated elegance. This styling is a reflection of who they are, their personal aesthetic, and the image they want to project on their big day.

2. Enhancing Natural Beauty:

Bridal makeup and hairstyling aim to accentuate a bride's natural beauty rather than mask it. The right techniques can bring out the eyes, define the cheekbones, and highlight every feature that makes the bride unique. It's about feeling like the best version of oneself.

3. Boosting Confidence:

When we know we look good, we feel good. The confidence that comes with professional hair and makeup is palpable. As a bride walks down the aisle, dances with her partner, and mingles with guests, the self-assuredness that she carries can significantly amplify the day's joy.

4. Symbolism and Tradition:

In many cultures, bridal hair and makeup carry symbolic meanings. For instance, in some traditions, specific hairstyles signify purity, good luck, or fertility. Makeup, too, can bear cultural significance, from the deep reds in Indian bridal looks representing excitement and passion to the white face makeup of Japanese brides symbolizing purity.

5. Ensuring Photogenic Results:

Weddings are extensively photographed events. Professional hair and makeup ensure that brides look their best not just in person but also in photographs that will be cherished for a lifetime. The right makeup can prevent issues like a shiny forehead, under-eye circles, or washed-out features in photos.

6. Setting the Day's Tone:

The bridal look can set the tone for the entire wedding. A boho-chic braided hairstyle and sun- kissed makeup can perfectly complement a beach wedding, while a sleek updo and dramatic makeup might suit a black-tie event. The bride's appearance can be a visual cue for the event's ambiance.

7. An Act of Self-care:

The process of getting one's hair and makeup done can be therapeutic. Amid the hustle and bustle of wedding preparations, sitting down for a makeup session or hair styling can offer a moment of relaxation and pampering.

8. Crafting Lasting Memories:

Long after the wedding is over, when the music has faded and the guests have left, the memories remain. How a bride looked and felt on her wedding day becomes an integral part of these memories. Every time she looks at her wedding photos or videos, her bridal beauty will remind her of the emotions, the excitement, and the love that defined that day.

In essence, bridal hair and makeup are not just about aesthetics. They are interwoven with emotions, traditions, and personal narratives, playing a pivotal role in the wedding journey. It's a blend of art, tradition, and personal expression, making it a crucial aspect of the bridal experience.

- Setting the Tone: Emphasizing Personal Style

The saying "first impressions last" might be old, but it remains relevant, especially when applied to weddings. The moment a bride enters, all eyes are on her, and her appearance sets the tone for the entire event. More than just the dress or the veil, the bride's hair and makeup choices play a pivotal role in emphasizing her personal style and, by extension, the mood of the wedding. Here's a deeper exploration of the importance of setting the tone through personal style:

1. Manifestation of Individuality:

Every bride is unique, bringing her tastes, experiences, and personality to her big day. The choices she makes regarding her hair and makeup are clear representations of her individuality. Whether she's an avant-garde bride opting for neon eyeshadow or a classic bride with a timeless red lip, these choices are personal declarations of who she is.

2. Personal Style as a Storyteller:

A bride's style choices narrate a story. They can hint at her journey, her passions, and her relationship. For instance, a bride might choose a retro hairstyle as a tribute to the era when her parents met or wear a particular shade of lipstick because it's the one she wore on her first date with her partner.

3. Crafting the Wedding's Ambiance:

The bride's personal style directly influences the ambiance of the wedding. A bride with a boho- chic look might suggest a laid-back, free-spirited celebration, while a bride with a sleek, modern appearance could hint at a more sophisticated and contemporary event.

4. Emotional Resonance:
Embracing personal style can have deep emotional resonance. It ensures that the bride feels authentic and true to herself. Instead of bending to fleeting trends, prioritizing personal preferences can enhance the bride's comfort and confidence.

5. A Guiding Beacon for Guests:
Believe it or not, guests often take cues from the bride. Her personal style can serve as a guide for guests, helping them gauge the formality of the event, understand its thematic undertones, and even influence their behavior and interactions throughout the celebration.

6. Navigating Cultural Nuances:
For many brides, personal style becomes a harmonious blend of individual choices and cultural traditions. For instance, a bride might wear traditional jewelry but pair it with a modern hairstyle. These choices emphasize the beautiful interplay between personal preference and cultural heritage.

7. Enhancing Cohesiveness:
A bride's personal style can bring cohesiveness to the wedding. By ensuring her hair and makeup align with other elements—like the dress, decor, venue, and even the invitations—there's a seamless flow to the event, making it more aesthetically pleasing and memorable.

8. Legacy of Memories:
Years down the line, when a bride looks back at her wedding photos, her style choices will evoke memories. Emphasizing personal style ensures that these memories remain evergreen, reminding her not just of the day but of the person she was at that moment.

In the grand tapestry of a wedding, personal style is more than just an aesthetic choice. It's a powerful tool of expression, setting the event's tone, weaving stories, and creating lasting impressions. It serves as a bridge between the bride's individuality and the collective experience of those present, making the day truly unforgettable.

II. Haircare Before the Wedding

Hair Analysis: Determining Your Hair Type and Needs

Your hair is as unique as your fingerprint. It carries a distinctive combination of texture, thickness, strength, and moisture level. For brides, understanding these attributes is crucial to create a perfect hairdo for the big day. But beyond weddings, a thorough hair analysis offers a wealth of knowledge, guiding daily hair care and styling practices. Here's a deeper dive into the importance of hair analysis and how to determine your hair type and needs:

1. The Basics of Hair Typing:

Hair types are commonly categorized based on their natural texture and curl pattern:

- **Type 1 (Straight):** Straight hair lacks a defined curl pattern and often shines more due to the even distribution of natural oils.

- **Type 2 (Wavy):** Wavy hair has a soft, S shaped curl pattern.

- **Type 3 (Curly):** Curly hair forms clear ringlets or spirals.

- **Type 4 (Coily/Kinky):** This hair type forms tight coils, curls, or zigzags.

2. Porosity - The Moisture Meter:

Porosity refers to your hair's ability to absorb and retain moisture. Hair can be low, medium, or high porosity:

- **Low Porosity:** Hair has a tight cuticle layer, making it challenging for moisture to enter.

- **Medium Porosity:** Hair can maintain a balanced moisture level.

- **High Porosity:** Hair easily absorbs moisture but struggles to retain it, often due to damage or processing.

3. Density - The Hair Population:

Density considers the number of individual hair strands on your scalp. Some have thick (high density) hair, while others might have thin (low density) hair.

4. Thickness - The Width of Individual Strands:

Thickness evaluates the diameter of individual hair strands. Hair can be fine, medium, or coarse.

5. The Scalp's Health:

A healthy scalp is essential for strong, luscious locks. Factors like oil production, dandruff, and scalp sensitivity play a significant role in overall hair health.

6. Recognizing Specific Needs:

Once you've deciphered your hair type and its properties, you can pinpoint its specific needs:

- **Hydration Needs:** Curly, coily, and high porosity hair often crave more moisture.

- **Protein Balance:** Hair that's stretchy or limp might benefit from protein treatments.

- **Protection Requirements:** Fine hair and damaged hair may need more protection from environmental stressors.

7. The Benefits of Hair Analysis:
Understanding your hair type and its specific needs can revolutionize your hair care regimen:

 - **Customized Care:** Tailored hair products and treatments ensure optimal health and appearance.

- **Cost-Effective:** Avoid wasting money on unsuitable products.

- **Time-Saving:** Reduce trial-and-error in product selection and styling methods.

8. Professional Consultation:
While self-assessment tools and quizzes can provide a basic understanding, consider consulting a professional trichologist or hairstylist for a detailed hair analysis. They can offer insights into hair health, potential issues, and recommend appropriate care and products.

9. Bridal Implications:
For brides, an accurate hair analysis ensures:

- **Optimal Health:** Hair in its best condition will look radiant on the wedding day.

- **Styling Compatibility:** Knowing hair type and needs assists in selecting a hairstyle that not only looks good but also lasts throughout the celebration.

- **Tailored Hair Trials:** Avoid multiple trials and errors, ensuring the chosen style is in harmony with the hair's natural tendencies.

In essence, hair analysis is akin to understanding a personalized manual for your tresses. With this knowledge in hand, you can navigate the world of hair care and styling with confidence, ensuring your locks remain healthy, vibrant, and stunning.

Hair Treatments: From Deep Conditioning to Protein Treatments

Your hair, often described as your crowning glory, requires consistent care and maintenance. Like a garden, it flourishes best when nourished and tended to with love. Over time, various factors like environmental pollutants, heat styling, chemical treatments, and daily wear and tear can compromise the health and appearance of your locks. Enter the world of hair treatments— designed to restore, rejuvenate, and elevate the condition of your hair. Let's delve into some of the most popular treatments and their benefits:

1. Deep Conditioning Treatments:

* Purpose: To hydrate and nourish the hair, restoring lost moisture.

* Ingredients: Often contain oils, butters, and humectants that attract and seal in moisture.

* Benefits: Improves elasticity, reduces breakage, adds shine, and softens hair.

* Application: Typically applied after shampooing, left on for an extended period (usually under a heat cap or steamer), and then rinsed out.

2. Protein Treatments:

* Purpose: To strengthen hair and repair damage.

* Ingredients: Contain proteins or protein hydrolysates like keratin, silk, wheat, or collagen.

* Benefits: Reduces breakage, fortifies hair structure, and restores elasticity.

* Application: Used after shampooing and usually require a follow-up with a moisturizing conditioner, as protein can sometimes feel stiff or brittle on the hair.

3. Hot Oil Treatments:

* Purpose: To impart moisture, shine, and suppleness.

* Ingredients: Natural oils like coconut, olive, argan, almond, or jojoba.

* Benefits: Seals cuticles, adds shine, promotes scalp health, and combats dryness.

* Application: Oils are warmed (not hot) and applied to hair and scalp, then covered with a plastic cap and left on for a duration, followed by rinsing.

4. Scalp Treatments:

* Purpose: To address specific scalp concerns like dandruff, oiliness, or itchiness.

* Ingredients: Can include salicylic acid, tea tree oil, peppermint oil, or other targeted ingredients.

* Benefits: Promotes a healthy scalp environment, which can lead to healthier hair growth.

* Application: Applied directly to the scalp, massaged in, and rinsed out or left in, depending on the treatment type.

5. Olaplex and Bond Builders:

* Purpose: To repair disulfide bonds in the hair compromised during coloring or other chemical processes.

* Ingredients: Active ingredients that work at a molecular level to rebuild hair's internal structure.

* Benefits: Strengthens hair from within, prevents damage during chemical processes, and improves overall hair integrity.

* Application: Can be mixed in with hair color or used as a stand-alone treatment.

6. Clarifying Treatments:

* Purpose: To remove product buildup, excess oils, and impurities.

* Ingredients: Strong surfactants and sometimes chelating agents.

* Benefits: Leaves hair feeling refreshed, revived, and free from heavy buildup.

* Application: Applied like a shampoo but used infrequently due to its stripping nature.

7. Hair Smoothing and Straightening Treatments:

* Purpose: To reduce frizz, straighten, and smooth hair for an extended period.

* Ingredients: Chemicals that change the hair's structure, like formaldehyde (used in some treatments) or amino acids.

* Benefits: Provides a sleek, frizz-free appearance for weeks or even months.

* Application: Applied by professionals, these treatments often involve a combination of product application, heat, and setting.

8. Hair Gloss and Glaze Treatments:

* Purpose: To add shine and sometimes a hint of color.

* Ingredients: Transparent or tinted formulas with shine-enhancing agents.

* Benefits: Provides a luminous shine, seals cuticles, and can enhance or tone color.

* Application: Applied after shampooing and conditioning, left on for a short duration, then rinsed.

In conclusion, hair treatments offer a smorgasbord of solutions tailored to various hair concerns. Incorporating them into your routine ensures that your tresses remain healthy, resilient, and radiant. For brides, these treatments can be game-changers, ensuring their locks look impeccable for their big day. Always remember to conduct patch tests or consult with a hair professional before diving into new treatments to ensure they're suitable for your specific hair type and needs.

The Importance of Trimming and Regular Salon Visits

Hair, as with every part of our body, undergoes wear and tear. No matter how meticulous we are with our hair care regimen, external factors such as pollution, UV radiation, physical manipulation, and even natural growth patterns can impact its overall health and appearance. This is where the significance of regular trims and salon visits comes into play. Let's dive into a more profound understanding of their importance:

1. Split Ends & Breakage:

* Manifestation: The ends of hair strands, being the oldest parts, are prone to splitting and breaking due to exposure and age.

* Trimming Solution: Regular trimming removes split ends, preventing them from traveling up the hair shaft and causing more extensive damage.

* Salon Insight: Professional hairstylists can identify early signs of split ends and trim them appropriately, ensuring hair retains its strength and vitality.

2. Maintenance of Shape and Style:

* Natural Growth Patterns: As hair grows, layers can grow out, bangs can lose their shape, and the overall style can appear unkempt.

* Trimming Solution: Periodic trims ensure that the chosen hairstyle retains its shape, volume distribution, and overall aesthetics.

* Salon Insight: Hairstylists can recommend tweaks to the original style based on hair growth and changing textures, ensuring the style remains fresh and flattering.

3. Hair Health Checks:

* Underlying Issues: Scalp conditions, early signs of hair thinning, or changes in hair texture can sometimes go unnoticed at home.

* Salon Advantage: Regular salon visits allow professionals to monitor the hair and scalp's health, potentially catching and addressing issues before they escalate.

4. Stimulation of Hair Growth:

* Growth Plateaus: Some believe that their hair has stopped growing when it reaches a certain length. Often, this isn't a halt in growth but rather breakage at the ends that counteracts the growth from the roots.

* Trimming Solution: Trimming encourages healthier, fuller-looking hair, giving the illusion of faster growth as the ends remain intact.

5. Refreshing Look and Boosting Confidence:

* Natural Evolution: Over time, personal style, age, or even facial features may change.

* Salon Advantage: Regular visits allow for periodic updates to hairstyles, ensuring the look remains current, flattering, and aligns with individual evolution. A fresh cut or style can also provide a significant boost in confidence and mood.

6. Product Build-up & Hair Residue:

* Accumulation: Over time, even with regular washing, product residue, pollutants, and minerals from water can accumulate on the scalp and hair.

* Salon Solution: Deep cleansing treatments at salons can effectively remove this build-up, allowing hair to breathe, shine, and absorb nutrients better.

7. Professional Hair Care Advice:

* Changing Needs: As we age, or as seasons change, hair needs can shift.

* Salon Insight: Regular interactions with hairstylists ensure that you're kept abreast of the best products, treatments, and practices tailored to your hair's evolving needs.

8. Therapeutic Experience:

Beyond the technical aspects, there's something inherently therapeutic about a salon visit. The act of being pampered, the tactile sensation of a scalp massage, and the transformative power of a fresh cut or style play a pivotal role in self-care and mental rejuvenation.

In essence, while home care is vital for hair health, the expertise, tools, and treatments available at a salon complement and elevate this care. For those looking to maintain the integrity, beauty, and health of their locks, incorporating regular trims and salon visits into their routine is not just a luxury but a necessary act of hair love.

DIY Hair Masks and Treatments

In an age where natural and organic treatments are gaining traction, DIY hair masks stand as a testament to the power of homemade remedies. Harnessing ingredients often found in kitchen cupboards or local markets, these masks offer a holistic approach to hair care, addressing a range of concerns from dryness to lack of shine. Here's an in-depth look at DIY hair masks and treatments, and how they can nourish, protect, and rejuvenate your tresses.

1. Why Opt for DIY Hair Masks?

- Natural Ingredients: DIY masks are typically free from artificial preservatives, colors, and fragrances. This means fewer chemicals on your scalp and hair.

- Cost-Effective: Making masks at home can be a wallet-friendly alternative to store-bought treatments.

- Customization: Adjust ingredients based on your hair's unique needs and concerns.

- Eco-Friendly: Reduce plastic packaging waste by using and reusing home containers.

2. Popular DIY Hair Mask Ingredients and Their Benefits:

- Banana: Rich in potassium, vitamins, and natural oils, it moisturizes and softens hair.

- Eggs: A protein-rich source that strengthens hair follicles and adds shine.

- Honey: A natural humectant, it attracts moisture and adds a lustrous shine.

- Coconut Oil: Penetrates hair shafts, providing hydration and reducing protein loss.

- Yogurt: Contains lactic acid which cleanses the scalp and proteins that strengthen hair. - Aloe Vera: Soothes the scalp, combats frizz, and promotes hair growth.

3. DIY Hair Mask Recipes:

* For Dry and Damaged Hair:

Mix 2 tablespoons of coconut oil, 1 ripe banana, and 1 tablespoon of honey. Apply to hair, let sit for 30-40 minutes, then wash off.

* For Oily Hair:

Combine 1/2 cup of yogurt with the juice of one lemon. Apply the mixture to the scalp and hair. Leave it on for 20-30 minutes and rinse.

* For Hair Growth:

Blend 2 tablespoons of aloe vera gel with 1 tablespoon of castor oil. Massage onto the scalp and hair. Leave for 40 minutes and rinse.

* For Shine and Smoothness:

Whisk 1 egg with 1 tablespoon of olive oil and 1 tablespoon of honey. Apply from root to tip, wait for 30 minutes, then shampoo and rinse.

4. Application Tips:

- Start Clean: Begin with detangled and slightly damp hair.

- Sectioning: Divide hair into sections for even application.

- Focus on Needs: If your ends are dry, concentrate the mask there. If the scalp is oily, focus more on the roots.

- Heat It Up: For deeper penetration, wrap your hair in a warm towel or wear a shower cap.

- Rinse Thoroughly: Ensure all residues are washed out to avoid build-up.

5. Precautions:

- Patch Test: Before applying any new ingredient, do a patch test to ensure no allergic reactions.

- Freshness: Use fresh ingredients to avoid introducing bacteria to the scalp.

- Avoid Over-Proteinizing: Too much protein can make hair brittle. If you're using protein-rich ingredients (like eggs), don't overdo it.

- Lemon Caution: If using lemon, avoid direct sunlight post-application as it can lighten hair or cause sensitivity.

6. Beyond Masks - DIY Scalp Treatments:

- For Dandruff: Mix equal parts of apple cider vinegar and water. After shampooing, apply the solution to your scalp, let it sit for 10-15 minutes, then rinse.

- For Scalp Stimulation: Combine a few drops of peppermint or rosemary essential oil with a carrier oil like jojoba or coconut oil. Massage onto the scalp for increased circulation and potential hair growth.

In summary, DIY hair masks and treatments offer a customizable, eco-friendly, and natural approach to hair care. With a world of ingredients at your fingertips, you can explore, experiment, and discover the perfect concoction tailored to your hair's specific needs. Remember always to listen to your hair, adjust treatments as necessary, and revel in the joy of self-crafted pampering.

III. Hairstyles

Trends Through the Ages: Historical Bridal Hairstyles

Hair has always been a vital component of beauty and self-expression, with bridal hairstyles being particularly symbolic across different cultures and eras. Over time, these styles have evolved, reflecting societal changes, technological advances, and artistic movements. Let's take a retrospective journey through the annals of history to explore the evolution of bridal hairstyles.

1. Ancient Egypt (c. 3000-30 BC):

- Tresses and Tiaras: Brides often wore their hair long and straight, adorned with headbands made of fresh flowers or metal.

- Extensions and Wigs: For wealthier brides, intricate wigs and hair extensions made from human hair or sheep's wool were popular.

2. Ancient Greece (c. 500-323 BC):

- Flowing Locks: Brides preferred their hair loose, flowing, and decorated with flowers and ribbons.

- Braided Updos: Intricate braids were crafted and pinned up, representing the knotting or "tying" of the marriage.

3. Ancient Rome (c. 509 BC-476 AD):

- Seni Crines: The most traditional Roman bridal hairstyle consisted of six braids crafted in a particular pattern,

resembling the six Vestal Virgins, symbolizing purity and chastity.

- Crowns and Veils: Brides often wore a yellow veil, called the "flammeum," and a floral or metal crown.

4. Medieval Europe (c. 500-1500):

- Crowned Affair: Young, maiden brides wore their hair loose as a sign of purity, often topped with simple crowns or circlets.

- Concealed Hair: Married women typically kept their hair concealed under veils or fabric hoods, showcasing modesty.

5. Renaissance (c. 1300-1600):

- High Foreheads: The beauty standard of this era favored a high, broad forehead. Brides often plucked or shaved the front part of their hairline to achieve this look.

- Braided Coronets: Hair was braided and wrapped around the head in a halo-like fashion, sometimes interwoven with pearls and jewels.

6. Victorian Era (c. 1837-1901):

- Demure Styles: Reflecting the modesty of the age, brides favored low buns, chignons, and simple updos, often adorned with flowers or veils.

- Ringlets: Loose, cascading ringlets framing the face became fashionable, representing femininity and grace.

7. Roaring Twenties (1920s):

- The Bob: With the flapper movement, short bobbed hair became a rage, even for brides.

- Finger Waves: This meticulous style, characterized by 'S' shaped waves held close to the head, became the go-to for many brides.

8. Golden Age of Hollywood (1930s-1950s):

- Glamour Waves: Inspired by silver screen divas, many brides opted for voluminous, glossy waves.

- Elegant Updos: Chignons and intricate updos, often with side-swept bangs or a flower, became popular.

9. Psychedelic Sixties (1960s):

- Beehives and Bouffants: Volume was key, with many brides choosing tall, teased hairstyles.

- Free-spirited Locks: As the decade progressed, the hippie movement brought about long, free- flowing styles adorned with flowers.

10. Modern Era (1970s-Present):

- Varied Inspirations: From the feathered styles of the '70s, big hair of the '80s, sleek straight looks of the '90s, to the tousled waves of the 2000s, bridal hair has seen a multitude of trends.

- Personal Expression: Today's brides are more eclectic, often blending historical inspirations with contemporary flair, prioritizing personal expression and individuality.

In conclusion, bridal hairstyles are more than just trends. They're a reflection of cultural norms, societal shifts, and individual personalities. As the ages have passed, brides have continuously used their hair as a canvas to convey beauty, tradition, rebellion, and self. In the current age, with the world's historical palette at their fingertips, brides have never

had more inspiration from which to draw and express their unique bridal vision.

Contemporary Bridal Hairstyles: A Deep Dive

In today's world of personalized weddings, bridal hairstyles have become a blend of traditional elegance and contemporary chic. Drawing inspiration from various eras and global influences, contemporary brides now have a plethora of styles to choose from. Let's delve deeper into some of the most popular contemporary bridal hairstyles:

1. Updos:

* Classic Chignon: A sophisticated style that screams elegance. The chignon can be sleek for a timeless look or slightly tousled for a more modern feel.

* Twisted Bun: Sections of hair are twisted and pinned, creating a dimensional and intricate bun that adds volume and flair.

* High Ballerina Bun: Positioned at the crown of the head, this style exudes grace and is perfect for brides looking for a chic, pulled-together look.

* Accessorized Updo: Embellishments like jeweled pins, flowers, or tiaras can be incorporated to elevate the overall aesthetic.

2. Half-up Half-down:

* Boho Waves: Soft waves paired with a half-tied style, usually with twisted or braided sections, offers a bohemian and romantic feel.

* Pouf Volume: A teased crown, reminiscent of the 60s, gives height and drama to the style.

* Cascade Curls: Luscious curls that flow down the back, with the top section pinned up, often with floral or jeweled accessories.

3. Loose Styles:

* Beachy Waves: Effortless, tousled waves for a relaxed yet polished look that's perfect for beach or outdoor weddings.

* Old Hollywood Glam: Glossy, side-parted waves that cascade down one shoulder, echoing the vintage charm of silver screen divas.

* Straight and Sleek: A minimalist look where hair is straightened to perfection, shining with health and gloss.

4. Braids:

* Crown Braids: Hair braided in a halo-like fashion around the head, offering a regal and ethereal look.

* Fishtail Braid: A modern twist on the traditional braid, the fishtail adds texture and intricacy, often draped over one shoulder

* Braided Updo: Braids aren't just for loose hair. Intricate braided buns or chignons provide a unique blend of tradition and modernity.

* Waterfall Braid: A semi-open braid where sections of hair cascade down, mimicking the flow of a waterfall.

5. Short Hair:

* Pixie with Panache: A well-styled pixie cut adorned with hairpins or a headband offers a chic, avant-garde look.

* Bobbed Beauty: Waves, curls, or straightened, bobs can be styled in numerous ways and accessorized with clips, bands, or even subtle extensions.

* Volumized Updo: Even short hair can be teased and pinned into a faux updo, especially with the help of extensions.

* Slicked Back: Using gel or pomade for a sleek, wet look adds edge and sophistication to a contemporary bridal style.

In essence, contemporary bridal hairstyles are a testament to the limitless creativity of modern brides. Whether inspired by eras gone by, global influences, or personal quirks, today's hairstyles embrace both individuality and tradition. With the right hairstylist and vision, a bride can craft a look that truly mirrors her essence, making her special day even more unforgettable.

Hairstyles Based on Themes: Crafting Your Perfect Bridal Look

Every bride dreams of a hairstyle that complements her wedding theme and encapsulates the essence of her personality. Aligning your hairstyle with your wedding theme creates a cohesive and harmonious aesthetic for the event. Here's a detailed exploration of hairstyles tailored to various wedding themes:

1. Beach Weddings:

* Effortless Waves: Embrace the natural sea breeze with loose, tousled waves that give a relaxed, sun-kissed vibe.

* Braided Crown: A crown braid adorned with tiny seashells or pearls invokes the spirit of the sea while keeping hair away from the face.

* Low Messy Bun: Casual yet elegant, this style pairs perfectly with a beach backdrop, allowing for the addition of tropical flowers or accessories.

2. Vintage-Inspired:

* Victorian Updo: Reflecting the 19th-century elegance, think intricate low buns or chignons adorned with vintage hairpins or combs.

* Flapper Waves: Channel the 1920s with short, defined finger waves, perfect for brides with bobbed hair.

* Hollywood Glam: Emulate 1940s and 1950s movie stars with deep side parts and glossy, cascading waves.

3. Bohemian Bliss:

* Loose Braids: Side braids, fishtails, or waterfall braids infused with wildflowers scream boho chic.

* Half-up Twists: Twisted sections pulled into a half-up style, complemented by loose waves or curls, exude a free-spirited vibe.

* Floral Crown: A headpiece made of wildflowers, greenery, or even dried flowers paired with loose hair, either straight or wavy, captures the bohemian essence.

4. Classic Elegance:

* Sleek Chignon: A timeless hairstyle, the chignon (low bun) embodies grace when styled sleekly at the nape of the neck.

* Audrey Hepburn Bun: A high bun, paired with a tiara or headband, is reminiscent of iconic classic beauties.

* Structured Curls: Elegantly positioned curls, either pinned up or cascading down, provide a refined and polished look.

5. Rustic Romance:

* Braided Updo: Perfect for a barn or countryside wedding, braids interwoven into an updo, adorned with rustic accessories like twigs or baby's breath, fit the theme beautifully.

* Low Ponytail: A loosely tied ponytail, either straight or wavy, adorned with a simple floral arrangement, mirrors the simplicity of rustic charm.

* Messy Bun: This effortless look, paired with small flowers or greenery, aligns perfectly with a rustic setting.

6. Modern Minimalist:

* Slicked Back Ponytail: A low or high ponytail with a sleek, gelled look exudes modern sophistication.

* Straight and Sleek: Long, pin-straight hair, perhaps with tucked behind one ear and adorned with a singular statement piece, resonates with minimalist design.

* Simple Bob: Short hair styled in a precise bob with clean lines epitomizes the minimalist aesthetic.

7. Fairytale Fantasy:

* Voluminous Curls: Think of princess-like voluminous curls cascading down, potentially paired with a tiara or sparkly headpiece.

* Intricate Braids: Braids interwoven with ribbons or studded with gems can create a hairstyle fit for royalty.

* Regal Updo: High, intricate buns or updos, complemented by regal accessories, make for a dreamy, fairytale look.

In summary, your wedding theme acts as a canvas, and your hairstyle is one of the masterstrokes that brings the picture to life. By aligning your hair with your theme, you can create a harmonious and memorable aesthetic that stands the test of time in both memories and photographs. Whether you're a beachy bride or dreaming of a vintage affair, there's a perfect hairstyle waiting to complete your vision.

Deciding Factors: Crafting the Perfect Bridal Hairstyle

Choosing the right bridal hairstyle is not just about personal preferences or current trends. Multiple factors play a pivotal role in making sure your hairstyle complements the overall bridal look. Here's a detailed exploration of the primary factors you should consider when deciding on your perfect bridal hairstyle:

1. The Dress:

* Silhouette and Style: A ball gown might call for a grander, more traditional hairstyle like a high bun or updo. In contrast, a sheath or slip dress might pair beautifully with relaxed waves or a sleek ponytail.

* Detailing: If your dress boasts intricate back details, consider an updo to show them off. A simpler dress might allow for more elaborate hairdos or accessories.

2. The Veil:

* Length and Style: A birdcage veil often pairs well with vintage hairstyles like finger waves or a chic bob. Longer veils, such as

chapel or cathedral lengths, may require sturdy updos to anchor them or can be draped elegantly over flowing locks.

* Attachment Point: Consider where the veil will attach. A veil that sits atop the head suits voluminous updos, while one that attaches at the base works with both updos and long styles.

3. Jewelry:

* Earrings: Statement earrings may necessitate simpler hairstyles, like a sleek chignon or tucked- behind-the-ear

waves, so they can shine. Daintier earrings might allow for more detailed and elaborate hairdos.

* Headpieces: Tiaras, crowns, or other headpieces require hairstyles that accommodate and complement them without overshadowing their beauty.

4. Neckline:

* Strapless or Sweetheart: These necklines offer versatility. You could opt for romantic curls, an elegant updo, or anything in between.

* High Neck: Given the covered nature of this neckline, consider an updo or a side-swept style to avoid overwhelming the dress.

* V-neck: Loose waves, half-up styles, or even braids can beautifully complement the V shape, adding balance and symmetry.

5. Face Shape:

* Round: Updos with volume on top or loose waves can elongate the face. Avoid hairstyles that add width around the cheeks.

* Oval: This balanced face shape can pull off a variety of styles, from updos to flowing locks.

* Square: Soft waves or curls can soften the jawline. Side parts or side-swept bangs can also complement this face shape.

* Heart: Voluminous styles, especially around the jawline, can balance the narrower chin. Avoid heavy volume on the crown or hairstyles that are slicked back tightly.

* Long: Styles that add width, like out-curled bobs or voluminous curls, work well. Updos should have volume on the sides rather than height on top.

In essence, achieving the perfect bridal hairstyle is a harmonious blend of various elements. While your desires and personal style should be at the forefront, considering the dress, veil, jewelry, neckline, and face shape ensures a balanced, cohesive, and flattering look on your big day. The key is to ensure that every element works in tandem, making you feel both beautiful and true to yourself.

IV. Hair Trials

Hair Trials: Navigating the Journey to Your Perfect Bridal Hairstyle

When envisioning your wedding day, everything from the gown to the shoes, and of course, the hairstyle plays a pivotal role in shaping that dream. Hair trials offer a bridge from this dream to reality. They're more than just a pre-wedding rendezvous with your hairstylist; they're an integral part of ensuring you look and feel your best. Let's dive deeper into the multifaceted world of hair trials.

Purpose and Importance of Hair Trials:

1. Eliminating Guesswork:
The main purpose of a hair trial is to remove any ambiguity. It provides a clear roadmap of what to expect, ensuring the wedding day hair process is streamlined and efficient.

2. Suitability:
While a hairstyle might look stunning in a magazine, it might not necessarily suit your face shape or hair texture. Trials let you test and decide.

3. Preventing Disasters:

Imagine discovering on your wedding day that your hair doesn't hold curls well or that a certain product makes your scalp itch. Trials help avoid such unforeseen issues.

Working with a Stylist:

1. Communication is Key:

Your stylist isn't just a service provider; they're your collaborator. Openly discuss your desires, concerns, and any ideas you might have. Bring along photos or sketches that inspire you.

2. Trust their Expertise:

While it's your vision, remember that stylists bring a wealth of experience. They can offer suggestions on what might work best given your hair type, length, and the wedding's overall theme.

3. Prepare for the Trial:

Arrive with your hair in its natural state, avoiding heavy products. This gives the stylist a blank canvas and a true sense of your hair's behavior.

Documenting Your Trials:

1. Comprehensive Photography:

Have photos taken from multiple angles – front, back, both sides, and even top-down. This not only helps you evaluate the look comprehensively but also provides a reference for the stylist on the wedding day.

2. Lighting Matters:

Ensure photos are taken in good lighting, preferably natural. This gives a realistic view of how your hair will look in daylight during the ceremony.

3. Accessorize:

If you're planning on wearing a veil, tiara, or any hair accessories, bring them to the trial. This allows for accurate photo documentation of the complete look.

Making Changes and Adjustments:

1. Speak Up:

If there's something you're uncertain about, voice it. It's easier to make adjustments during a trial than on your wedding day.

2. Trial Round Two:

If after the first trial, you're considering a different hairstyle altogether, don't hesitate to schedule a second trial. It's essential to feel confident in your choice.

3. Fine-tuning:

Sometimes, minor tweaks, be it in volume, placement of accessories, or the lightness of curls, can make a world of difference. Work with your stylist to refine the details.

In conclusion, hair trials are an essential phase in the wedding prep process, ensuring that on the big day, there are no surprises – at least not with your hair. By effectively collaborating with your stylist and methodically documenting the process, you pave the way for a hairstyle that not only complements your aesthetics but also feels intrinsically 'you'. Remember, it's not just about looking beautiful; it's about feeling beautiful, confident, and truly in the moment as you say, "I do."

V. Day-of Hair

Day-of Hair: A Comprehensive Guide to Bridal Hair Perfection

The day you've been eagerly awaiting is finally here – your wedding day! While the journey to this point has been filled with planning and trials, the day itself comes with its own set of guidelines. Here's a detailed exploration of how to manage your day-of bridal hair to ensure that everything goes off without a hitch.

Prepping Your Hair:

1. Start with a Clean Slate:

Wash your hair the night before with a sulfate-free shampoo. This helps remove any buildup without overly stripping the hair, making it more manageable.

2. Avoid Over-conditioning:

While it might seem tempting to use a heavy conditioner for silky tresses, it can sometimes make hair too soft and slippery to hold certain styles. Stick to a lightweight conditioner.

3. Natural Drying:

Avoid using heat tools on the morning of. Instead, let your hair air dry if possible. This minimizes damage and retains its natural texture, which can aid in styling.

4. Product Application:

On the advice of your stylist, use a heat protectant if you'll be using curling or straightening irons. A lightweight mousse can also provide volume and hold.

The Role of Hair Accessories:

1. Tiaras:

A symbol of elegance and royalty, tiaras demand hairstyles that are equally regal. Ensure the tiara sits securely, aligning with the style, be it atop a voluminous updo or a cascade of curls.

2. Hairpins:

These are versatile accessories, perfect for adding subtle glimmers of beauty. Scatter them throughout a braided crown or use them to secure a chignon.

3. Vines:

Perfect for boho and garden weddings, hair vines weave seamlessly into braids and twists, giving a whimsical touch.

4. More Accessories:

From combs to barrettes to fresh flowers, ensure each accessory complements your hairstyle, dress, and overall theme. Remember, less is often more; don't overcrowd your hair.

Ensuring Longevity: Products and Techniques:

1. Setting Sprays:

Choose a high-quality hairspray that promises hold without making hair crunchy. It should withstand the elements, especially if you're having an outdoor wedding.

2. Layering Products:

For added security, layer products. Start with a volumizing product, add a texturizing spray for grip, and finish with a setting spray.

3. Consider the Climate:

If you're in a humid environment, opt for anti-frizz products. In dry climates, hydrating serums or oils can prevent hair from looking parched.

4. Touch-up Kit:

Have a small kit with bobby pins, hairspray, and a comb for touch-ups throughout the event.

Emergency Fixes:

1. Flyaways:

Carry a toothbrush sprayed with hairspray to tame any unruly strands without disturbing the rest of your hairstyle.

2. Drooping Curls:

A mini curling iron or wand can be a lifesaver. Have your bridesmaid or a friend on standby for quick fixes.

3. Hair Accessory Malfunction:

If a pin or accessory comes loose, having extra hairpins and a mini tube of super glue can save the day.

4. Static Control:

In a pinch, a dryer sheet can be run over your hair to control static. It's a quick and effective fix.

In essence, the key to immaculate day-of bridal hair lies in meticulous preparation and having contingencies for unforeseen hair mishaps. When paired with the craftsmanship of a trusted stylist and the support of your bridal party, you're well on your way to looking and feeling your best as you step into this new chapter of life.

VI. Skincare Before the Wedding

Skincare Before the Wedding: A Comprehensive Approach to Radiant Bridal Skin

The glow that emanates from a bride is unparalleled, a blend of happiness, excitement, and undoubtedly, impeccable skincare. Skincare, in the months leading up to the wedding, is not just about products and treatments; it's a holistic approach encompassing routines, diet, and targeted solutions. Let's delve into the nuances of pre-wedding skincare to ensure that you shine brilliantly on your big day.

Skincare Routines Based on Skin Type:

1. Oily Skin:

- Cleansing: Opt for a gel-based or foaming cleanser that effectively removes excess oil without over-drying.

- Toning: A mattifying toner can help regulate oil production.

- Moisturizing: Use a lightweight, oil-free moisturizer to keep skin hydrated without adding shine.

- Exfoliation: Regular exfoliation, preferably with salicylic acid, can keep pores clear and reduce breakouts.

2. Dry Skin:

- Cleansing: Cream-based cleansers will cleanse without stripping the skin of its natural oils.

- Toning: A hydrating toner will restore skin's pH and moisture balance.

- Moisturizing: A richer moisturizer, or even facial oils, will deeply nourish dry skin.

- Exfoliation: Gentle exfoliation with lactic acid or a hydrating scrub will remove flaky skin, revealing a smoother texture.

3. Combination Skin:

- Cleansing: A balanced cleanser that isn't too drying or too oily is ideal.

- Toning: Consider targeted toning, using a mattifying toner for oily areas and a hydrating one for dry patches.

- Moisturizing: Lightweight, balancing moisturizers work best.

- Exfoliation: Regular exfoliation will ensure both oily and dry areas are addressed.

4. Sensitive Skin:

- Cleansing: Gentle, fragrance-free cleansers will prevent irritation.

- Toning: A soothing toner with ingredients like chamomile or rose water is beneficial.

- Moisturizing: Fragrance-free, hypoallergenic moisturizers are a must.

- Exfoliation: Opt for very gentle, hydrating exfoliants and use less frequently.

Facials: Which Ones and How Often?

1. Hydrating Facials: Ideal for dry or dehydrated skin, these can be done monthly.

2. Deep Cleansing Facials: For those with oily or acne-prone skin, consider this facial every 3-4 weeks.

3. Brightening Facials: Targeting pigmentation and dullness, these can be scheduled every month.

4. Gentle Facials: For sensitive skin, opt for soothing facials every 4-6 weeks.

5. Advanced Treatments: Microdermabrasion, chemical peels, or laser treatments should be started at least 6 months prior, with consultations from a dermatologist.

Addressing Skin Concerns:

1. Acne: Regular facials, topical treatments, and in some cases, medications can be used. Always consult with a dermatologist.

2. Pigmentation: Topical brightening products, vitamin C serums, and advanced treatments like chemical peels can address dark spots and uneven tone.

3. Scarring: Microneedling, dermal fillers, or laser treatments might be necessary, initiated well in advance of the wedding.

The Role of Diet and Hydration:

1. Hydration: Drinking ample water not only flushes out toxins but also ensures skin remains plump and radiant.

2. Balanced Diet: Incorporate a diet rich in fruits, vegetables, lean proteins, and whole grains. These foods contain vitamins and antioxidants that promote skin health.

3. Limit Sugar and Dairy: Excess sugar can lead to skin aging, and for some, dairy can trigger breakouts. Consider reducing their intake.

4. Omega-3s: Foods rich in omega-3 fatty acids, like flaxseeds, walnuts, and fatty fish, can help improve skin texture and reduce inflammation.

In conclusion, the path to radiant bridal skin is a mix of tailored skincare routines, professional treatments, and holistic lifestyle choices. Starting early and being consistent will pave the way for skin that's not just wedding-ready, but healthier in the long run. After all, as you embark on this new journey, it's not just about the day, but also the many beautiful days that follow.

VII. Makeup Styles

Makeup Styles: From Timeless Elegance to Contemporary Trends

Makeup, with its transformative power, has evolved over the centuries. For brides, makeup is an extension of their personality, a reflection of the times, and often a nod to tradition. Here's a detailed journey through the world of bridal makeup, from historical milestones to the freshest contemporary trends.

Makeup Through History: Iconic Bridal Looks

1. Ancient Egypt: Queens and noblewomen adorned their eyes with kohl and green malachite eye shadows. Lips and cheeks tinted with red ochre signified status and allure.

2. Renaissance Era: Pale skin was a hallmark of beauty and privilege. Women would powder their faces with white lead, and their cheeks and lips with crimson.

3. 1920s: The flapper era brought dramatic eyes, thin arched brows, and deep red lips. This was an era of breaking norms and emphasizing a woman's independence.

4. 1950s: Inspired by Hollywood, the 50s saw the popularity of winged eyeliner, red lips, and defined brows, reminiscent of icons like Marilyn Monroe.

5. 1980s: Bold was the keyword. Think vibrant eyeshadows, heavy blush, and glossy lips.

Contemporary Bridal Makeup Styles:

1. Natural:

- **Overview:** Less is more. This style emphasizes the bride's natural beauty with subtle enhancements.

- **Key Features:** Light foundation, nude eyeshadows, a touch of mascara, and a soft lip tint.

How-to:

1. Base: Start with a hydrating primer for a smooth canvas. Follow up with a light to medium coverage foundation.

2. Eyes: Use neutral-toned eyeshadows. Mascara should be applied for subtle length, not dramatic volume.

3. Cheeks: A light blush in a shade that mimics your natural flush will work wonders.

4. Lips: Go for lip tints or nude shades that complement your skin tone.

Beauty Tips:

- Ensure your skin is well-moisturized before makeup application.

- Use a setting spray to keep the makeup in place, ensuring the natural look lasts all day.

2. Glamorous:

- **Overview:** Perfect for the bride who wants to shine and stand out.

- **Key Features:** Smokey eyes, full coverage foundation, contouring, and a bold lip color. Highlighting is essential to achieve that radiant finish.

How-to:

1. Base: Begin with a mattifying primer. Opt for a full coverage foundation.

2. Eyes: Play with deeper shades for a smokey eye look. Add eyeliner and voluminous mascara. False lashes can amplify the glam.

3. Cheeks: Contouring is key. Highlight the high points of your face for a radiant finish.

4. Lips: Bold shades of red, wine, or berry can be used.

Beauty Tips:

- Always blend your contour well to avoid harsh lines.

- Using a lip liner before the lipstick can help achieve a precise and long-lasting lip look.

3. Vintage:

- **Overview:** Drawing inspiration from past eras, especially the 20s, 50s, and 60s.

- **Key Features:** Depending on the era, it could be a bold red lip, winged eyeliner, or dramatic lashes.

How-to:

1. Base: A primer to smooth imperfections. Medium to full coverage foundation.

2. Eyes: Depending on the era, you could go for winged eyeliner or subtle shimmery shadows.

3. Cheeks: Rosy blushes work best to achieve that vintage flush.

4. Lips: Classic red or deep pinks, paired with a lip liner for a defined look.

Beauty Tips:

- For that 1950s look, use a liquid eyeliner for a sharper wing.

- A matte finish lipstick will transport you to the vintage era more authentically.

4. Cultural/Traditional:

- **Overview:** Rooted in various global traditions, this makeup style honors heritage.

- **Key Features:** In India, for instance, brides opt for heavy kohl eyes and red lips. In parts of East Asia, subtlety and porcelain finishes are preferred.

How-to:

1. Base: Depending on the cultural preference, this could range from light to full coverage.

2. Eyes: Some cultures prefer heavy eyeliner, while others might lean into bright eyeshadows.

3. Cheeks: Blush shade will vary based on cultural nuances.

4. Lips: From deep reds to soft pinks, this varies widely based on tradition.

Beauty Tips:

- Do your research on specific cultural makeup preferences. Some might have a preference for gold-toned makeup, others might prefer jewel tones.

- Consider cultural accessories; they play a huge role in the overall look. For example, bindis in Indian culture or intricate facial paintings in certain African cultures.

Makeup Based on Themes and Seasons:

1. Beach Weddings:

- **Look:** Sun-kissed and glowing.

- **Key Features:** Bronzed cheeks, shimmer eyeshadows, and a coral lip. Waterproof makeup is essential.

2. Winter Weddings:

- **Look:** Ethereal and frosty.

- **Key Features:** Pale eyeshadows, a touch of blush, deep berry lips, and lots of highlighter for that snow-kissed glow.

3. Bohemian:

- **Look:** Earthy and dreamy.

- **Key Features:** Soft brown and gold eyeshadows, peach lips, and a hint of blush.

4. Classic/Traditional:

- **Look:** Timeless elegance.

- **Key Features:** Neutral eyeshadows, winged eyeliner, red lips, and a soft contour.

In conclusion, bridal makeup is a beautiful tapestry of the past, present, and personal. Whether a bride leans towards the understated grace of the 'natural' look, the vibrant energy of 'glamorous' makeup, or the deep-rooted significance of 'cultural' styles, her choice paints a story. With the ever-evolving world of makeup, she has a plethora of styles to choose from, ensuring that on her special day, she feels both beautiful and authentically herself.

VIII. Makeup Trials

Makeup Trials: A Deep Dive into Perfecting Your Bridal Look

Weddings are one of the most photographed events in a person's life. Naturally, every bride desires makeup that not only complements her but also withstands the test of time (and flash photography). Enter makeup trials – a series of sessions that help brides and makeup artists find that 'just right' look. Let's delve into the intricacies of makeup trials and why they are quintessential.

The Need for Multiple Trials:

Why More Than One?

1. Versatility: Multiple trials allow you to explore a variety of looks, from natural and vintage to glamorous and cultural.

2. Different Conditions: One trial can be done during the day, another In the evening. This helps in understanding how makeup reacts under varying light conditions.

3. Refinement: Each trial offers an opportunity to refine and perfect the previous look.

4. Peace of Mind: Multiple trials ensure you and the makeup artist are on the same page, reducing potential day-of stress.

Documenting Each Look:

Why Document?

1. Visual Reference: Photographs provide a concrete reference for both you and the artist.

2. Feedback Loop: Sharing the documented look with friends and family can offer valuable feedback.

3. Durability Check: Documenting how the makeup wears over a few hours helps gauge its longevity.

How to Document?

- Take pictures in different lighting conditions: natural daylight, indoor lighting, and flash. - Capture various angles: front, side profiles, and close-ups of detailed work.

- Use a high-quality camera for clarity.

Allergies and Sensitivities: Patch Testing

Why is Patch Testing Crucial?

1. Safety First: The last thing any bride needs is an allergic reaction.

2. Identifying Culprits: If there's a reaction, you can pinpoint the specific product causing it.

3. Ensuring Comfort: Apart from allergies, some products may simply feel uncomfortable on the skin.

How to Patch Test?

- Apply a small amount of product (especially foundation, primers, and skincare) to the inner wrist or behind the ear.

- Wait for 24 hours. If there's redness, itching, or any discomfort, that product is a no-go.

Adjusting Based on Feedback:

The Value of Feedback:

1. Objective Opinions: Sometimes, a third person can offer insights you or the makeup artist might miss.

2. Refinement: Constructive feedback helps in tweaking and achieving the desired look.

3. Confidence Boost: When your chosen circle affirms the look, it boosts confidence in your final makeup decision.

How to Seek and Implement Feedback:

- Share documented pictures with a trusted group: could be close friends, family, or even co- workers.

- Be open to suggestions, but also trust your gut feeling.

- Relay the feedback to the makeup artist and collaborate on adjustments.

In essence, makeup trials are not mere rehearsals. They are collaborative sessions that pave the way for a bride's envisioned look to come to life. Through meticulous planning, open communication, and a touch of exploration, brides can ensure that when they walk down the aisle, their makeup is nothing short of perfection.

IX. Day-of Makeup

Day-of Makeup: Ensuring Your Radiance Shines All Day Long

Your wedding day is a culmination of months, sometimes years, of planning. Every moment is precious, and naturally, every bride wishes to look her best from the moment she steps onto the aisle till the final dance. Ensuring that your makeup remains impeccable throughout this whirlwind requires strategic application and the right products. Let's delve into the essentials of day-of makeup.

The Importance of Priming:

Why Prime?

1. Smooth Canvas: Primers fill in pores, fine lines, and imperfections, giving makeup a smooth surface to adhere to.

2. Longevity: It ensures that the makeup lasts longer, reducing the need for frequent touch-ups. 3. Color Vibrancy: Eye and lip primers can make colors pop and appear more vibrant.

Tips for Priming:

- Choose a primer suitable for your skin type.

- Allow the primer to sit for a few minutes before applying foundation.

Foundations: Matching and Longevity

Foundation Fundamentals:

1. Shade Match: It's essential to pick a shade that matches your skin tone and undertone perfectly.

2. Coverage: Depending on your preference and skin's needs, choose between light, medium, or full coverage.

3. Long-wearing Formulas: For weddings, opt for foundations labeled long-wear or stay-proof.

Tips for Foundation:

- Always test foundation shades in natural light.

- Blend foundation down the neck to avoid any stark lines.

- Use a setting powder to lock the foundation in place.

Eye Makeup: From Shadow to Lashes

Eyes That Captivate:

1. Eyeshadow: Consider waterproof and smudge-proof formulas. Neutral tones are timeless, but don't shy away from colors if they match your theme.

2. Eyeliner: Waterproof gel or liquid eyeliners ensure longevity.

3. Mascara: Waterproof mascara is a must, considering the emotional moments that might lead to teary eyes.

4. Lashes: False lashes add drama. Choose natural-looking ones or go dramatic based on your look.

Eye Makeup Tips:
- Use an eyeshadow primer to enhance the color and longevity of the shadow. - Consider individual lashes for a more natural look.

Lips: Long-lasting Choices

For Lips that Don't Fade:

1. Lip Liner: Outline and fill in lips with a liner to make lipstick last longer.

2. Matte Formulas: They generally last longer than glossy ones.

3. Layering: Apply, blot, and reapply to ensure staying power.

Lip Tips:

- Pick a shade that complements your overall makeup look.

- Carry your lipstick for touch-ups, especially after eating or drinking.

Final Touches: Highlighting, Contouring, and Setting

Mastering the Final Touches:

1. Highlight: Accentuate the high points of your face – cheekbones, brow bone, and the bridge of the nose.

2. Contour: Define your cheekbones, jawline, and nose for a more sculpted look.

3. Setting: Lock in your makeup with a setting spray. This step ensures that makeup stays put.

Tips:

- Blend, blend, blend! Whether it's your highlight or contour, blending ensures a seamless look. - Choose a setting spray suited to your skin type.

Emergency Touch-ups

Even with all the precautions, having an emergency kit is wise.

What to Include:

1. Blotting papers to combat shine.

2. Q-tips for smudge fixes.

3. Your lipstick for reapplications.

4. Translucent powder for any shine or oil. 5. Mini setting spray for freshness.

In essence, day-of makeup is an art and science combined. It's not just about creating a beautiful face, but also about ensuring that beauty remains untouched as you make memories. With the right products, techniques, and a touch of foresight, every bride can ensure she looks as radiant at the end of the day as she did at the start.

X. Professional Help vs. DIY

Professional Help vs. DIY: Navigating Your Bridal Beauty Choices

For many brides, deciding whether to enlist the help of a professional makeup artist and hairstylist or to opt for a DIY approach is a critical decision. Both paths have their merits, and the choice often comes down to personal preferences, budgetary constraints, and the bride's level of skill and comfort. Here's a deep dive into each option.

Benefits of Hiring Professionals:

1. Expertise: A professional brings years of training and experience. They're adept at tailoring makeup and hair to suit individual features, skin types, and personal styles.

2. Stress Reduction: On your big day, having someone else take care of your beauty needs can alleviate stress.

3. Product Quality: Professionals usually invest in high-end products that are long-lasting and photograph well.

4. Tools and Equipment: From airbrushing to high-quality hair tools, professionals come equipped with items most people don't typically own.

5. Time Management: Professionals are accustomed to working under time constraints and can ensure you're ready in a timely fashion.

Cost Factors:

1. Professional Fees: Hiring seasoned professionals can be pricey. Costs can vary widely based on location, the reputation of the artist, and specific requirements.

2. Trial Sessions: Most professionals charge for trial sessions, though some might adjust this cost if you book them for the wedding.

3. Travel and Accommodation: If your chosen professional doesn't reside near the wedding location, you might need to cover their travel and accommodation.

DIY: Tutorials, Courses, and Practice:

1. Learning Resources: There's an abundance of online tutorials, especially on platforms like YouTube and Instagram, dedicated to bridal makeup and hair.

2. Taking Courses: For those serious about DIY, consider taking a short course. Many beauty schools offer them.

3. Practice: This can't be stressed enough. If you choose the DIY route, practice repeatedly. Remember, practice makes perfect.

4. Feedback: After practicing, seek feedback from trusted friends or family to refine your look.

DIY vs. Professional: A Comparative Analysis:

1. Cost: DIY can be more economical, especially if you already own quality makeup and hair products. However, remember that if you lack certain products, purchasing them might escalate costs.

2. Personal Touch: DIY allows you to have complete control over your look, ensuring it's 100% in line with your vision.

3. Skill Level: While tutorials are helpful, not everyone can achieve professional-level results, especially for intricate hairstyles or specific makeup techniques.

4. Time: Doing it yourself might take longer, especially without the practiced efficiency of a professional. Factor in potential redos.

5. Endurance: Professionals know tricks and techniques to ensure makeup and hair last all day and night. DIY brides need to research and test products for endurance thoroughly.

6. Experience: For some brides, the process of getting pampered by a professional is part of the wedding experience. For others, the satisfaction of crafting their look is a cherished part of their big day.

In Conclusion:

The choice between hiring a professional or opting for DIY comes down to what makes you feel most comfortable and confident. If you trust in your skills and enjoy the process of creating your look, then DIY could be for you. However, if you value the expertise, convenience, and potentially stress-free experience that a professional offers, that might be your best bet. Remember, every bride's ultimate aim is to feel her best, so choose the path that aligns with your vision, budget, and comfort level.

XI. Post-Wedding Care

Post-Wedding Care: Revitalizing Hair and Skin after the Big Day

The wedding day, with all its glory and beauty, can be demanding on your hair and skin. Hours of heavy makeup, intricate hairstyles, and the general whirlwind of the day can leave them both craving some TLC. Just as pre-wedding prep is crucial, post-wedding care is essential to rejuvenate and restore. Here's a guide to effective post-wedding care.

Haircare After Heavy Styling:

1. Gentle Cleansing:
- After hours of holding sprays, mousse, and possibly teasing, your hair needs a mild shampoo to cleanse without stripping natural oils. Consider a sulfate-free shampoo.

2. Deep Conditioning:
- A rich, nourishing conditioner or mask can help restore moisture balance. Leave it on for a longer duration for an added boost.

3. Avoid Heat:
- Your hair has likely endured heat styling for the wedding. Give it a break for a few days by avoiding straighteners, curling irons, and even blow dryers.

4. Natural Oils:
- A light application of oils like argan, coconut, or jojoba can help in restoring shine and health.

5. Trim if Necessary:
- If you feel like your hair underwent a lot of stress, consider a light trim to get rid of any split ends.

Makeup Removal: Do's and Don'ts:

Do's:

1. Double Cleanse:
- Start with an oil-based cleanser to break down heavy makeup, followed by a gentle foam or gel cleanser.

2. Use a Lip Remover:
- Long-lasting lip products can be stubborn. Use a dedicated lip makeup remover or a bit of oil.

3. Gentle Eye Makeup Removal:
- The skin around the eyes is delicate. Use a specialized eye makeup remover and gently wipe off, never rub.

Don'ts:

1. Avoid Alcohol-Based Removers:
- They can be drying and irritating, especially after a day of heavy makeup.

2. Don't Rush:
- Take your time to ensure all makeup is thoroughly removed.

3. Don't Forget the Hairline and Neck:
- Makeup and products can accumulate here, so ensure these areas are cleaned as well.

Skin Rejuvenation:

1. Exfoliate:
- A few days after the wedding, consider a gentle exfoliation to

get rid of dead skin cells. It helps in reviving the skin's natural glow.

2. Hydration Boost:
- Weddings can be dehydrating. Use hydrating masks, serums, or creams to restore moisture.

3. Calm and Soothe:
- If your skin feels irritated or shows redness post-wedding, products with ingredients like aloe vera, chamomile, or calendula can help soothe it.

4. Spa Day:
- A post-wedding spa day can be therapeutic. Opt for facials that focus on hydration and relaxation.

5. Maintain a Routine:
- After the wedding, continue with a regular skincare routine. It maintains the health and glow of the skin.

In Conclusion:

After the hustle and bustle of the wedding, it's time to pamper yourself. Prioritize post-wedding care to ensure that your hair and skin bounce back to their radiant best. With a little time and attention, you can ensure that the beauty of the wedding day has long-lasting effects.

XII. Expert Interviews

Expert Interviews: Gleaning Insights from the Pros

When it comes to bridal beauty, seeking advice from industry experts can be incredibly beneficial. They bring a wealth of experience and knowledge that can help brides achieve their best look. Here's a compilation of insights from hairstylists, makeup artists, and dermatologists.

Hairstylists: Tips and Tricks

1. Scalp Health is Key: Renowned hairstylists often emphasize the importance of a healthy scalp for lustrous locks. Regular scalp massages with nourishing oils can boost blood circulation and promote hair health.

2. Use the Right Products for Your Hair Type: Whether curly, straight, thick, or thin, each hair type has unique needs. Professional hairstylists often stress the importance of using products specifically designed for your hair type to get the best results.

3. Limit Heat Exposure: Continuous heat styling can damage hair. It's recommended to always use a heat protectant and take regular breaks from hot tools.

4. The Magic of Dry Shampoo: For volume and texture, especially in updos, many hairstylists swear by dry shampoo. It adds grip and helps hairstyles hold better.

5. Regular Trims: Even if growing out hair for the big day, regular trims prevent split ends and keep hair looking healthy.

Makeup Artists: Insights on Products and Techniques

1. Priming is Paramount: Almost every makeup artist will emphasize the importance of a good primer. It ensures makeup longevity and creates a smooth canvas.

2. Blend, Blend, Blend: The key to flawless makeup often lies in blending. Whether it's eyeshadow, foundation, or contour, blending ensures there are no harsh lines.

3. Know Your Skin Undertone: Choosing the right foundation or lipstick shade becomes easier when you know your undertone. Makeup artists often categorize undertones as cool, warm, or neutral.

4. Invest in Good Brushes: A high-quality brush can make a significant difference in application. Regular cleaning of these brushes is also crucial to prevent skin breakouts.

5. Setting is Crucial: Setting sprays and powders are often the unsung heroes in a makeup artist's kit. They ensure that makeup remains in place, come rain or shine.

Dermatologists: Healthy Skin Advice

1. Sun Protection Always: The harmful effects of UV rays are well-documented. Dermatologists uniformly advocate for daily sun protection, regardless of weather.

2. Hydration Inside-Out: Drinking ample water and using hydrating serums or moisturizers can keep skin plump and radiant.

3. Avoid Last-Minute Treatments: Dermatologists advise against trying new skin treatments close to the wedding day as there's a risk of reactions.

4. Know Your Skin Type: Skincare isn't one-size-fits-all. Dermatologists often emphasize the importance of using products suited to individual skin types.

5. Address Issues Early: Concerns like acne, pigmentation, or scars shouldn't be left for the last moment. It's always wise to consult with a dermatologist well in advance of the wedding.

In Conclusion:

The collective wisdom of hairstylists, makeup artists, and dermatologists can provide brides with a comprehensive approach to their beauty preparations. By paying heed to their expert tips and tricks, every bride can ensure she looks her absolute best on her big day.

XIII. Star Bridal Hair and Makeup Inspirations

When planning the perfect wedding look, brides frequently turn to the timeless elegance and trend-setting styles of celebrities. Hollywood's A-listers, royals, and top influencers have access to the best in the beauty industry, offering a plethora of inspiration for soon-to-be-brides. These star-studded weddings set the tone for bridal trends globally, and their iconic looks are often replicated, from red carpets to royal palaces.

1. Meghan Markle: Natural Elegance:

Meghan Markle's wedding to Prince Harry was a global spectacle, and her beauty choices did not disappoint. Opting for a natural, radiant look, she showcased her freckles with a sheer foundation, subtle smokey eyes, and a neutral pink lip. Her understated, messy bun, paired with a few loose face-framing tendrils, added a modern twist to royal bridal elegance. Meghan's look emphasized the beauty in simplicity, making her a beacon for brides who lean towards understated glamour.

2. Priyanka Chopra: Dual Culture Bridal Beauty:

When Priyanka Chopra tied the knot with Nick Jonas, she beautifully melded Western and Indian bridal looks. For her Christian ceremony, she wore a soft, romantic hairdo with long, loose waves cascading down her back, paired with a delicate veil. Her makeup was luminous with a hint of shimmer on the lids, rosy cheeks, and a bold berry lip. For the Hindu ceremony, she went traditional with a tight bun adorned with flowers, deep red lips, and striking eyes accentuated with kohl, showcasing the richness of Indian bridal makeup.

3. Hailey Baldwin: Classic and Contemporary:

Hailey Baldwin, when marrying Justin Bieber, managed to blend both classic and modern bridal beauty. Her hair, pulled back in a low bun with soft, wispy pieces around the face, exuded a timeless appeal. Makeup was fresh, with dewy skin, a light pink lip, and eyes highlighted with shimmering shades of champagne and soft brown.

4. Kim Kardashian: Hollywood Glamour:

For her extravagant wedding to Kanye West, Kim Kardashian epitomized Hollywood glamour. Her makeup featured her signature contoured face, smoldering smokey eyes, and nude glossy lips. Her sleek, middle-parted hair tucked behind her ears was a modern take on classic bridal hairstyles, allowing her statement-making Givenchy gown to shine.

5. Kate Middleton: Royal Regality:

Kate Middleton's wedding to Prince William was a defining moment in bridal trends. Her half-up, half-down hairstyle, set with soft waves, became an instant classic. A subtle tiara placed perfectly atop her head emphasized her new royal status. Kate's makeup was self-done, highlighting her natural beauty with rosy cheeks, a soft pink lip, and defined eyes. This look became a go-to for brides seeking a mix of tradition and modernity.

6. Solange Knowles: Avant-Garde Beauty:

Known for breaking the mold, Solange's wedding beauty was no exception. She embraced her natural hair, wearing it out in a glorious Afro, challenging traditional bridal hair norms. Her makeup was minimal, with a focus on strong brows and a nude lip, allowing her natural beauty and unique style to stand out.

7. Ciara: Bohemian Chic:

For her wedding to Russell Wilson, Ciara embodied bohemian beauty. Her hair, styled in loose waves and adorned with a simple crown, exuded a fairytale charm. Her makeup was ethereal, with a bronzed glow, soft smokey eyes, and a neutral lip, perfectly complementing her boho-chic aesthetic.

8. Bianca Jagger: 70s Icon:

Throwing it back to the 70s, Bianca Jagger's wedding to Mick Jagger remains iconic. Her slicked- back hair, paired with a wide-brimmed hat, was the epitome of cool. Her minimal makeup, with just a hint of a smokey eye and natural lips, showcased her confident beauty and remains a source of inspiration for brides looking for a retro edge.

9. Audrey Hepburn: Timeless Beauty:

Audrey Hepburn's wedding look for her marriage to Mel Ferrer remains one of the most iconic in history. Her short, pixie haircut was adorned with a flower crown, exuding innocence and charm. Her doe-eyed makeup, with voluminous lashes and bold brows, emphasized her captivating eyes. Audrey remains a symbol of elegance, with brides still replicating her timeless look.

10. Amal Clooney: Sophisticated Beauty:

Amal Clooney's wedding to George Clooney saw her embrace a sophisticated, classic beauty. Her voluminous, side-swept waves gave a nod to old Hollywood, while her makeup was impeccably elegant with bold lashes, a flawless base, and a bold red lip.

XIV. Conclusion

In conclusion, celebrity bridal beauty looks serve as a rich source of inspiration for brides worldwide. Whether leaning towards the understated elegance of royals or the glamorous allure of Hollywood, there's a star-studded look to fit every bride's dream. The key takeaway from these iconic beauties is authenticity. Each star, in their unique way, stayed true to their personal style, resulting in memorable looks that stood the test of time. As brides seek inspiration, the ultimate aim should be to feel their most confident, radiant self, making their wedding day truly unforgettable.

In the realm of bridal beauty, while celebrity inspirations provide a roadmap, the most heart-stopping looks invariably stem from a bride's genuine essence. It's this individuality, when paired with iconic styles, that creates a mesmerizing fusion of tradition and personal flair. Emphasizing the bride's individuality not only enhances her natural beauty but also ensures that her look remains timeless in photographs and memories.

Furthermore, as the big day approaches, it's crucial to have a last-minute beauty checklist on hand. This isn't just about the tangible – the lip color or hairpin – but also about the intangible. A moment of reflection, a deep breath, and a final mirror glance can work wonders for composure and confidence. Ensure that you have a mini touch-up kit, perhaps bestowed by a thoughtful bridesmaid, containing essentials like lipstick, blotting paper, and a compact mirror. Having these on standby can provide peace of mind and ensure you remain radiant throughout the proceedings.

Lastly, as you embark on this momentous journey, remember that beauty isn't solely defined by perfect hair or immaculate makeup. True beauty emanates from joy, love, and the promise of shared tomorrows. May your wedding day not just be the manifestation of dreams but also the beginning of countless cherished moments. Here's to love, laughter, and a lifetime of happiness!

Samantha Pretto